Disney
MOANA
Bracelet Book

EDDA USA

Introduction

From the time Moana was young, her father Chief Tui was certain she would become the next great leader of their beautiful green island of Motunui. But then, the crops began to fail and no fish were left in the lagoon. Chief Tui became angry when Moana suggested, against the rules of the island, that the people try fishing beyond the reef, and he demanded that his daughter stay away from the open sea.

That's when Gramma Tala revealed that Moana's ancestors were once adventurous voyagers — before the demigod Maui stole the life-giving heart of the mother island Te Fiti. Until someone forces Maui to return the heart, darkness will spread from island to island, chasing all the life away.

With Gramma Tala's encouragement to follow her passion, Moana sets sail across the ocean on a quest to find Maui and set things right with Te Fiti. Like the daring seafarers before her, she learns how to use the stars and waves to stay on course. Along the way, she learns to listen to her inner voice—and understand her own place in the world, with her people, with nature, and with herself.

The bracelets in this book are inspired by the resources and world around Moana, and are also a tribute to the innovative skills and customs passed down by generations of extraordinary Pacific Island wayfinders — like Moana!

Coconut Button Bracelet

For the people of Motunui, coconuts are much more than a delicious food. The villagers spin fibers from dried coconut husks into strong cords to bind the huts they live in and to snare the fish they catch. Sometimes, parts of the coconut are even turned into toys, such as spinning tops and kites. Here, etched coconut shell buttons strung on natural twine make a fun and pretty wristlet.

Coconut Button Bracelet

Materials:
24-inch length hemp or other natural fiber cord (10-lb. or 20-lb. weight)
30-inch length hemp or other natural fiber cord (thin enough to fit 2 strands through each button hole)
10 or more coconut husk buttons (5/8 inch in diameter)

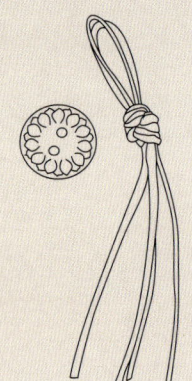

1 Line up the center of both cords, and tie an overhand knot to create a button-size loop.

2 Thread each of the two thin cord ends up through separate buttonholes.

3 Cross the thin threads over each other and thread the ends down through the opposite buttonholes.

4 Flip the bracelet over and tie the thin cords over the thicker cords and then under them to secure the button.

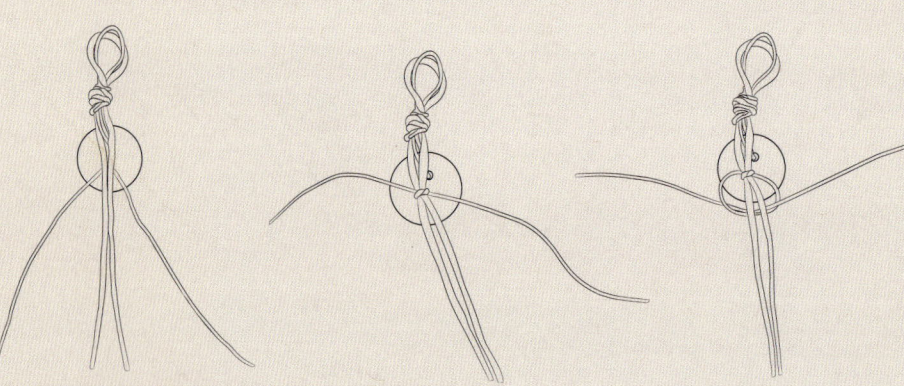

5 Add a second button and tie it in place.

6 Repeat until you've added enough buttons to wrap all the way around your wrist.

7 Tie all the cord ends together in an overhand knot below the last button. Make sure it is large enough to hold the bracelet on when slipped through the loop at the opposite end. Unravel the cord ends below the knot for a decorative look.

Sailor's Knot Bracelet

When Moana first sets out on her journey to restore the heart of Te Fiti, she tries to steer her boat toward a constellation that looks like a giant fishhook, but huge waves sweep her ashore on a small rocky island. That's where she finds the demigod Maui! Eventually, he agrees to teach her how to navigate by reading the swell of the waves and the position of the stars. In addition to being an accomplished navigator, she must also be a good sailor. That means knowing the proper way to lash the outrigger sail and exactly how to pull the paddle in order to stay the course. Like the tried-and-true hitches tied by the mariners of the Pacific Islands, this nautical bracelet is designed to hold fast wherever your journey takes you.

Sailor's Knot Bracelet

Materials:
Two 12-inch lengths thick (about ¼ inch) cotton cord
Thin natural fiber cord (small enough to thread through a button hole)
Small coconut husk, shell, or wooden button (about ⅝ inch in diameter)

1 Form a loop with the midsection of one of the thick 12-inch cords, crossing the right end over the left one.

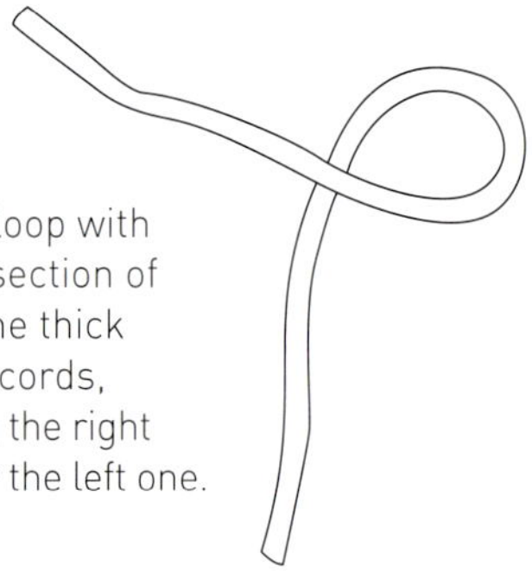

2 Loop the midsection of the other 12-inch length under the vertical tail of the first one, bringing the ends up over the loop and horizontal tail.

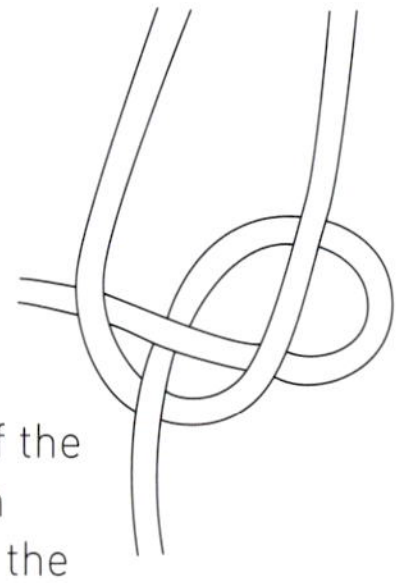

3 Thread the left end of the second length up through the top of the loop, then over itself, and back down through the bottom of the loop.

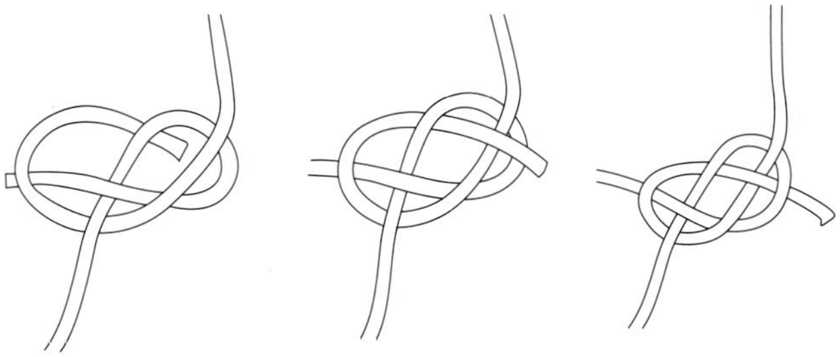

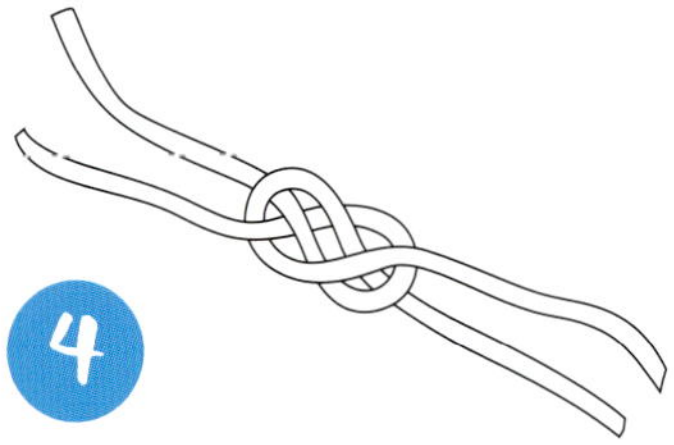

4 Gently pull the two sets of cord ends horizontally, adjusting the Sailor's Knot so that it is symmetrical and in the center of the cords.

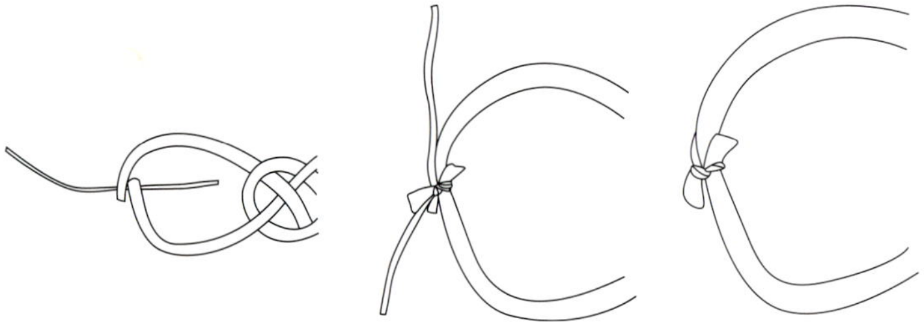

5 To create the loop fastener, slightly overlap the ends of the left set of cords and tie them together with a piece of the thin cord. Clip the ends close to the knot.

6

Bind the tied portion together. First, fold a 10-inch length of thin cord over a third of the way from one end, then place the folded portion on top of the knot. Starting about an inch below the knot, tightly wind the longer tail of the thin cord around the joined bracelet ends, working your way up and over the knotted portion. Then thread the end through the cord loop and gently but firmly pull the lower trailing end down until the little loop slides under the coils. Trim the ends.

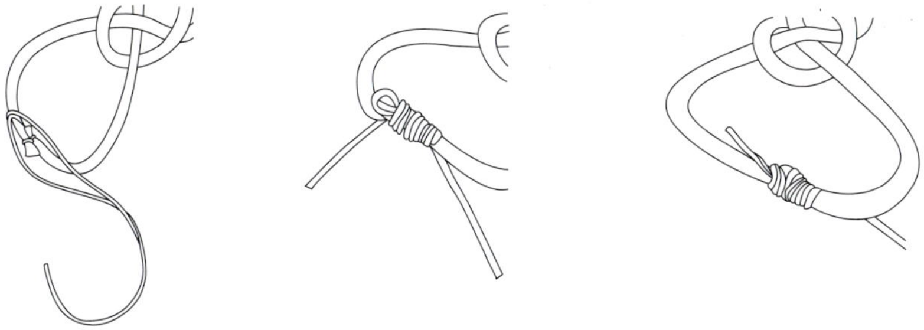

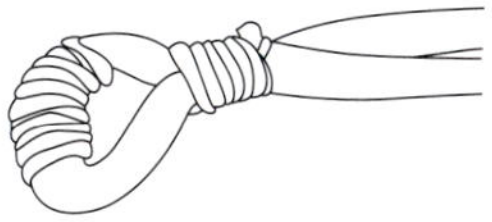

7

Use the same method from step 6 to bind the two bracelet cords together to create a loop just big enough for the button to slide through.

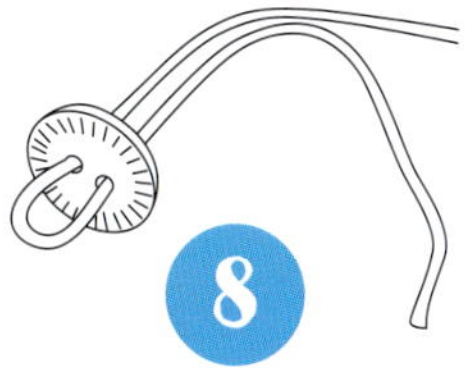

8

Thread a piece of the thin cord through the holes of the button.

9

Tie the button around the ends of the right set of cords. To fasten the bracelet, simply slip the button through the loop.

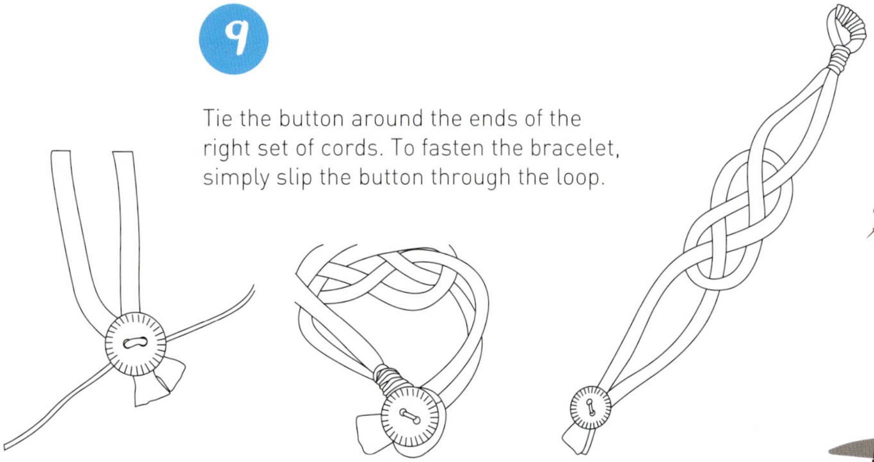

Decoupage Bracelet

While Moana's journey brings her face to face with terrifying monsters, at least the legendary shape-shifting demigod Maui is at her side. Not only does Maui know how to use his magical fishhook to slow down the sun and pull islands out of the sea, he is also covered with tattoos that tell the stories of his adventures. Literally! The images actually come to life on his skin. This decoupage bracelet craft, inspired by the Pacific Islanders' art of tattooing, lets you use decorative papers to create a motif of your very own.

Decoupage Bracelet

Materials:
Large wooden craft sticks (choose ones with straight grain)
Regular-size wooden craft stick
Craft paper (assorted solid colors and geometric patterns)
Tacky glue/glue sealer and small paintbrush for applying it

For a bracelet with a string back, you'll also need:
2 coconut husk buttons (5/8 inch in diameter)
Natural fiber yarn or string (thin enough to thread through the button holes)

 1

Soak several large craft sticks in a container of water for at least 30 minutes. Once the sticks are somewhat softened and pliable, very gently bend them with your fingertips to form curved cuffs that fit into a drinking glass.

Note: For a bracelet that stays on without a back strap, you'll need a narrower glass. Or you can wrap a rubber band or piece of yarn around the ends to hold a tighter shape.

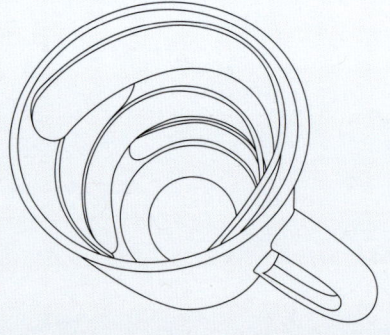
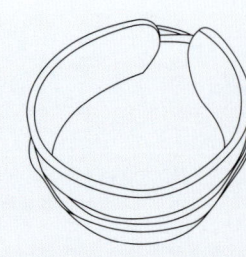

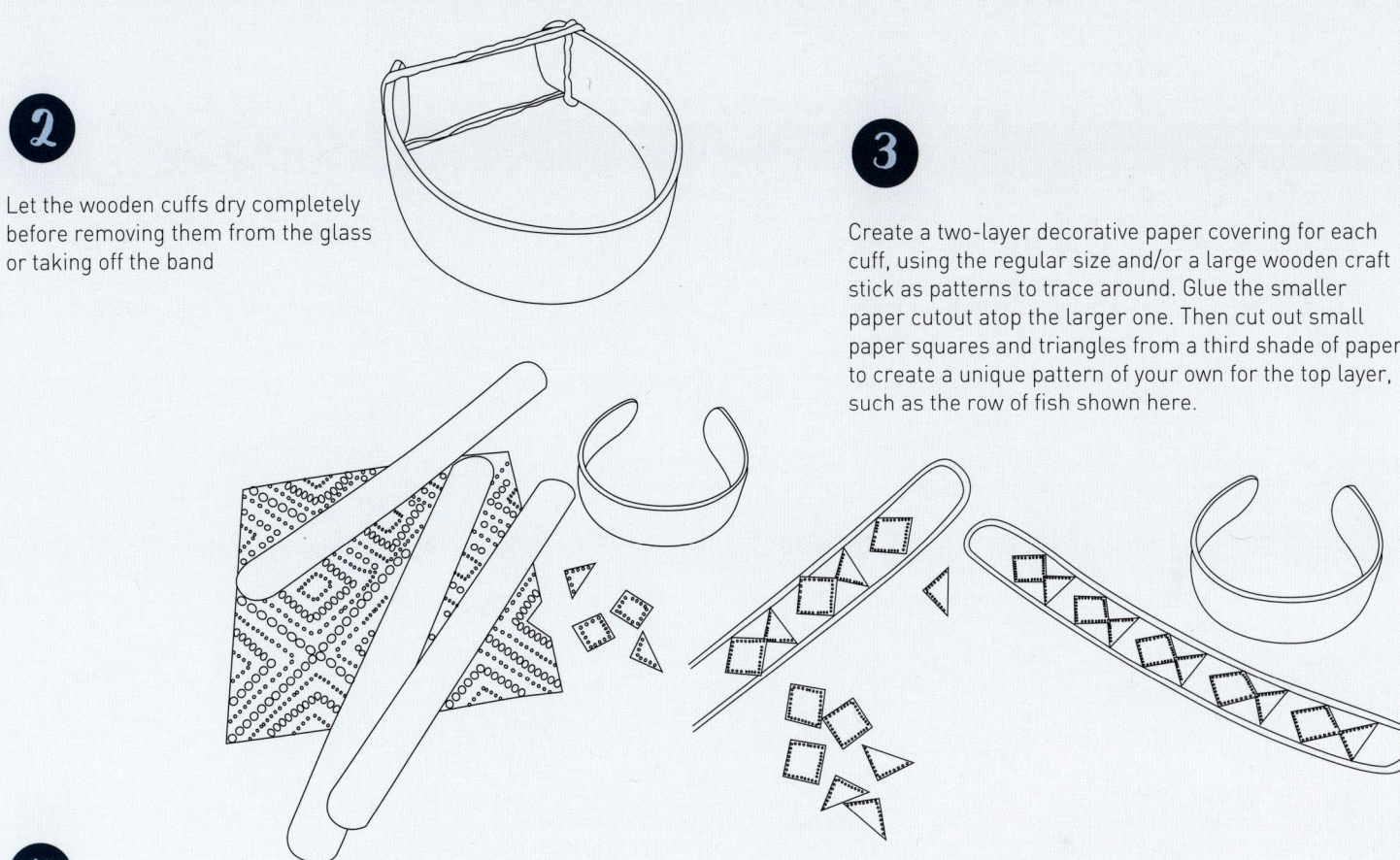

2

Let the wooden cuffs dry completely before removing them from the glass or taking off the band

3

Create a two-layer decorative paper covering for each cuff, using the regular size and/or a large wooden craft stick as patterns to trace around. Glue the smaller paper cutout atop the larger one. Then cut out small paper squares and triangles from a third shade of paper to create a unique pattern of your own for the top layer, such as the row of fish shown here.

4

Glue the assembled paper bracelet covering onto the face of the wooden cuff. Brush the entire cuff (inside and out) with a coat of diluted glue or glue sealer. Let it dry completely.

Note:
For a bracelet with a string back, thread the ends of a piece of yarn or cord down through the holes of each button, and tie them together at the back of the button. Glue the buttons to the outer ends of the bracelet. Once the glue is completely dry, tie the yarn or string ends together and trim them an inch or so from the knot. Unravel the ends beyond the knot to create a decorative fringed look.

Lauhala-style Bracelet

Pacific Islanders have long been exceptional weavers, splitting the leaves of native plants and trees to make all types of reeds. The hala (or pandanus) tree is a particular favorite for making plaited baskets, sleeping mats, and fans. Lauhala weaving can also be used to create amazing hats, stylish purses, and intricate multi-colored bracelets. Here's how you can use the lauhala technique to weave a striking two-tone bracelet from strips of raffia.

Lauhala-style Bracelet

Materials:
Raffia (natural and tinted)
Cardboard tissue or paper towel tube
Paper clips
Toothpick

1 For the bracelet base, cut open a tissue or paper towel tube. Then, flatten the cardboard, and cut two matching strips of cardboard the width of your desired bracelet.

2 Fit the two strips together, overlapping the ends to form a ring that will slip onto your wrist. Use pieces of raffia to tie the ends together.

3 For "reeds," cut a piece of raffia that is long enough to wrap one and a half times around the outer cardboard base. Cut additional matching lengths from the same shade of raffia until you have enough to cover the width of the cardboard when you place them side-by-side. Clip the raffia ends to the cardboard to hold them in place while you weave.

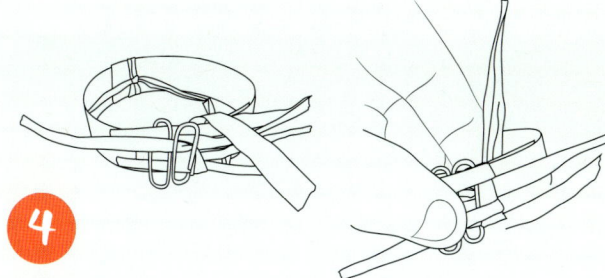

 4

Cut a length from the second shade of raffia that measures eight to ten times the length of the other reeds, and slip a 2-inch section of the end under the clips. Loop the reed through and around the band one time. Then fold every other short reed back over the wrapped reed.

5

Loop the long reed around the bracelet again, and bring the folded reeds forward over the second coil.

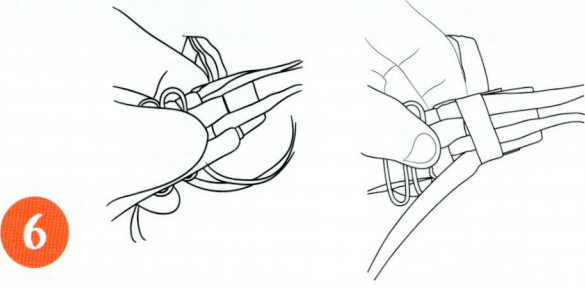

 6

Now, fold the opposite short reeds backward and then loop the long reed around the bracelet for the third time

7

Continue weaving in this manner all the way around the bracelet. Note: if the long reed isn't long enough, just tie another piece to the end and continue (you can tuck the ends under the weave when you finish). When you near the beginning, remove the clips and continue weaving right over the starting ends of the short reeds.

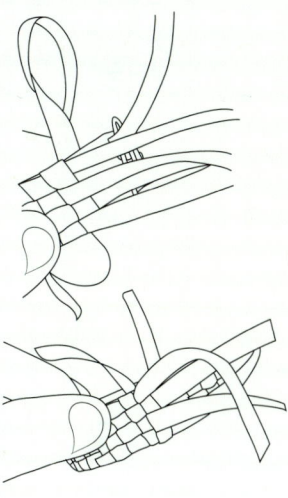

8

Separate the four short reed ends into two groups, pressing one pair to the left and the other pair to the right. Wrap the long reed around the bracelet between the two sets and then tie the ends together on the inside of the bracelet. Trim the ends to about ½ inch, and use the tip of a toothpick to tuck them under one or two nearby coils.

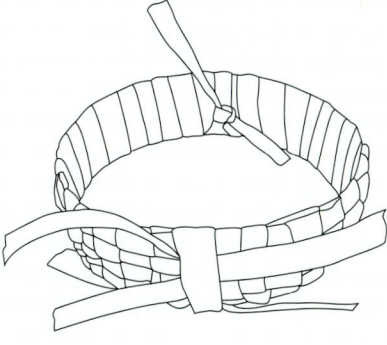

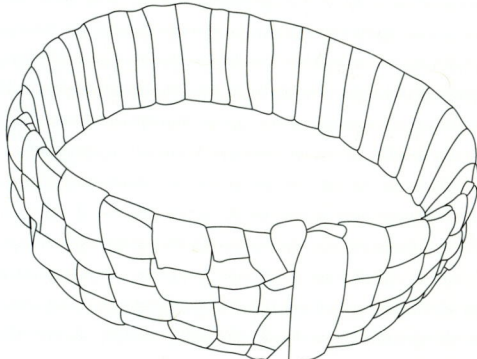

Spiral Bracelet

The red double spiral on Moana's outrigger sail is a special symbol for Moana and the people of Motunui. They believe the spiral moving inward symbolizes returning to the start, while the spiral moving outwards represents moving toward new beginnings. The same double spiral pattern is at the center of the bright green stone — Te Fiti's heart — that the ocean revealed to Moana when she was just a little girl. With a bit of clay and paint, you can fashion a spiral bracelet that will serve as a reminder to look inside yourself, to discover your inner voice, and then use that knowledge to take action outwards in the world.

Spiral Bracelet

Materials:
Off-white or tan polymer clay
Toothpick
Brown craft paint
Small paintbrush
Tissue or paper towel
Glue sealer
Off-white natural fiber cord (10-lb. weight)
Natural fiber tinted cord (15-lb. weight)
Coconut husk or shell button
(5/8 inch in diameter)

1

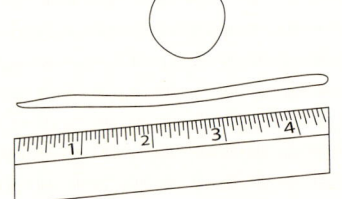

To make the spiral disk, start with a 3/8-inch ball of polymer clay and press it into a disk about 3/8 inch thick. Roll another bit of clay into a thin snake shape about 1/4 inch wide and 4 inches long, tapering the ends to points.

2

Loosely coil the snake into a spiral.

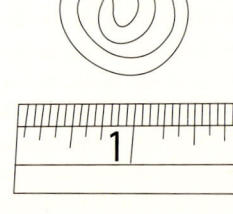

3

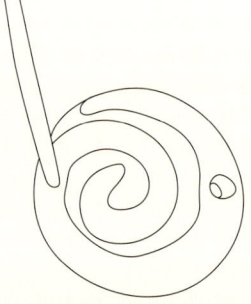

Set the spiral atop the clay disk and gently press down to stick it in place. Then, use a toothpick to make two holes 1/4 inch thick down through the clay on opposite sides of the disk. Tip: you can wiggle the inserted toothpick to broaden the holes.

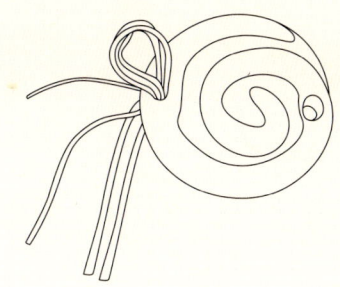

4

Bake the clay disk as specified in the manufacturer's directions. Once the clay has cooled completely, accent the recessed portion of the spiral with brown paint. Brush a lighter coat of paint on the raised portion as well and then blot the top with a bit of tissue or paper towel to give it a mottled antique look. Seal the entire disk with a coat of glue sealer, and let it dry completely.

5

Cut a 16-inch length from the off-white cord and a 36-inch length from the tinted cord. Line up the midpoints of both cords, then fold the doubled lengths in half and thread the fold up through one of the holes in the disk. Thread the ends through the loop and tighten the cinch.

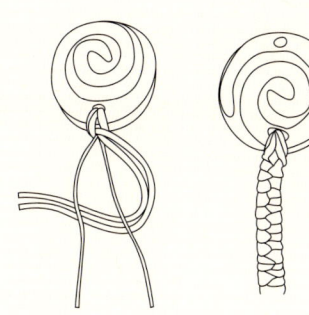

6

To create the bracelet band, gather the two tinted cords together on the right side, and weave them toward the left first going over the nearest thinner cord and then under the far one. Next, weave the tinted pair back toward the right, this time going over the nearest cord and under the next one. Tighten the tinted cords and slide them up toward the disk. Continue weaving back and forth in this manner until the band is long enough to reach halfway around your wrist (1¾ to 2¼ inches).

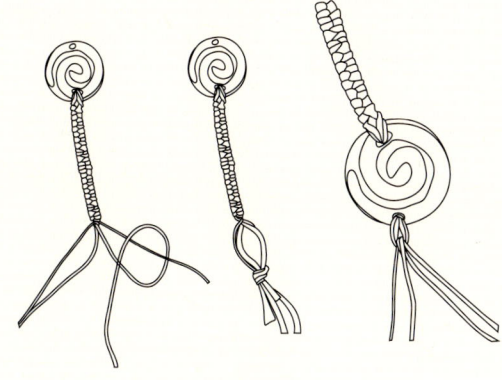

7

Tie the thinner cords tightly around the tinted ones. Tie the four strands together with an overhand knot about ¾ inch down from there to create the loop end of the bracelet fastener. Trim the ends below the knot and unravel them to create a fringed look.

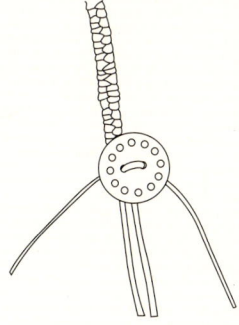

8

Create the other side of the bracelet band in the same way as the first, but instead of creating a loop at the end, attach a button. First thread the ends of the thinner cords up through the buttonholes, then cross them over each other and thread them down through the opposite holes. Tie the ends tightly around the tinted cords behind the button.

9

Trim and unravel the four strands below the button, and the bracelet is ready to wear.

Moana Bracelet Book

© 2016 Disney Enterprises, Inc. all rights reserved.

Author: Cynthia Littlefield
Bracelet illustrations: Aadarsh Put Ltd.
Layout and cover design: Baddydesign
Printed in USA

Distributed by Macmillan

All rights reserved. Published by Edda Publishing USA LLC.
No part of this book may be reproduced in any form or by any means, electronic or mechanical, including photocopying, recording, or by any information storage or retrieval system, without written permission from the publisher.

ISBN: 978-1-94078-757-2

www.eddausa.com